Whales

Amazing Facts & Pictures for Children on These Amazing Creatures

(Awesome Creature Series)

By Hathai Ross

Table of Contents

Introduction

Whales have long fascinated humans. They are very large - larger than any animal that lives on land. Despite their gigantic size, they are gentle creatures of the world's oceans. Over the years, people have learned to train some of these whales that have become permanent features in sea parks and water shows.

In this book, find out more about these magnificent creatures. Learn more about them such as what they eat, how the different kinds of whales look like, where they swim, and so much more.

Read this book and find out more astonishing facts about whales.

Chapter 1 Basic Facts About Whales

Whales are among the largest creatures that still live today. They are the larger relatives of the cute dolphins and porpoises. One of the things that get people surprised when they learn about whales is finding out that these huge creatures are mammals. Yes, mammals, like cats, dogs, apes, you and me. In fact, they, along with sea cows or manatees, are the only mammals that spend their whole lives in water, from the moment they are born until they die.

Types of Whales

There are basically 2 kinds of whales. There are baleen whales and toothed whales.

Baleen whales are whales that have a structure called baleen instead of teeth. This is composed of a row of very fine, coarse hair where the teeth should be. Whales use the baleen as a filter. Baleen whales open their mouths and gulp tons of sea or ocean water. When they close their mouths, water goes out through the fine hairs of the baleen structure in their upper jaw. The water is filtered, leaving behind tiny creatures called plankton, which is food for these whales. Aside from plankton, baleen whales are also able to filter small fishes and crustaceans (sea creatures with shells such as shrimps). Baleen whales are the largest whales that swim the world's oceans and seas. There are 10 different kinds of baleen whales.

Toothed whales have teeth, which look like large pegs. They eat larger sea and ocean animals like other marine mammals (seals, leopards, etc.), squid, fish and sometimes, other whales. Toothed whales use echolocation instead of eyesight when they swim or when they find food. Echolocation is using the echo of their voices to find out where they are, where the food is and where they are going. There are 66 different kinds of toothed whales.

General Characteristics

Whales share some important characteristics with other mammals. They breathe air, filling their huge lungs when they swim up to the surface of the water. They feed their babies with milk, just like how baby tigers and other baby mammals are fed. Also, whales have hair, although very little.

The bodies of whales are like those of fishes- long and streamlined. This allows them to swim easily. Their flippers are paddle-shaped, which also helps them to swim. The tail fins are also called flukes, which help in propelling or moving the heavy body of the whale through the waters. Some whale species have dorsal fins, or fins at their backs, which again, help with the swimming. Whales swim differently from fishes. Fishes swim by moving their tailfins from side to side. Whales move their flukes or tail fins up and down while they swim.

Whales have blubber. This is a layer of fat below their skin. This fat layer serves as a source of energy for the whale. It also serves as insulation, like a sweater that keeps the whales warm as they swim around the colder parts of the ocean.

Whales are warm-blooded animals. This means that their bodies must maintain a constant high temperature. This is where the layer of blubber comes in handy. The thick layer of fat helps to keep their bodies warm when they swim in cold waters, and protects their bodies from getting too warmed up by the temperature of the environment.

Blowholes are holes on top of the whale's head. This is where they breathe while they are underwater. There are 2 blowholes on top of baleen whales' heads, while toothed whales have only one.

What do whales eat?

Different kinds of whales eat different kinds of food. Some whales eat only the tiniest creatures, the plankton. Some eat larger animals, while some even eat other whales.

Where do whales go?

Whales swim all over the world. Where they go depends on the species. Some whales swim way up to the ice-covered North Pole. Some swim in warmer waters. Some swim in both cold and warm waters, depending on the time of the year and their age. Most whales swim to colder waters where they feed and then swim to warmer waters where they breed (find their mates and have their babies).

Some whales travel the vast oceans alone. Some travel in groups, called pods. Their traveling is called migration. Toothed whales are often found hunting in groups. They migrate together, sharing in their duties on rearing the young.

What do whales do besides swimming?

Whales may have massive bodies but they are quite active. They can jump high out of the water and come crashing into the water. This is called breaching. This is one of the unique activities observed among whales. In fact, even the massive humpback whale and other large whales breach.

Sometimes, whales can be seen thrusting or lifting their tails out of the water and slapping the water surface. This is believed to be a whale's way of sending out a warning that danger is nearby. Another way that whales communicate is through sounds or "whale song". These can be extremely loud. This way, the sound can travel for miles and be heard by other whales even when they are very far away.

Another unique trait among whales is conscious breathing. Most animals breathe without having to think about it or deciding when to breathe or when not to breathe. Whales are different. They decide when they will breathe. This helps them to control their breathing when they need to be underwater for a very long time. This is also the reason why whales cannot sleep for a long time because they have to remind themselves to swim up to the surface and breathe.

How do whales reproduce?

Time for whales to mate and breed depends on their species or kind. Some mate every year, some at longer intervals. A mother whale takes about 9 to 15 months before giving birth. A whale only gives birth to one baby every time.

Once a baby is born, he swims with his mom until he is old enough to hunt for food. This often means that baby whales swim with their mothers until they are more than 1 year old. During this time, they drink milk from their mother and strengthen their body as they grow.

Whales breed in warm parts of the oceans. Female whales give birth to 1 baby, called a calf, every 1 to 3 years. They only breed when their baby whales are already big enough to leave and hunt on their own. Baby whales are born with mottled colors, usually a mix of gray and black. This helps to camouflage or make them difficult for predators to see. Baby whales are born with very little hair covering their entire body. As they grow old, they also lose their hair.

FUN FACTS

Here are a few fun facts about whales:

- The biggest of all kinds of whales is the blue whale. It grows to as long as 29 meters or 94 feet, which is about the height of a 9-story building.

- The smallest of the whales is the dwarf sperm whale. The full-grown size is 2.6 meters or 8.5 feet long.

- The fastest whales are shortfin pilot whales and killer whales. They can swim as fast as 48 kph (kilometers per hour) or 30 mph (miles per hour).

- The longest migration is made by gray whales. They travel as long as 12,500 miles every year.

Unique Whale Behaviors

Breaching

As mentioned, whales breach. They swim upwards towards the surface of the water, jump high out of the water and then come crashing down, slapping the water. Experts believe that whales do this for fun, part of their playtime. Sometimes, whales breach in order to loosen the parasites on their skin. Whale experts also believe that sometimes, whales use breaching to communicate with other whales.

Spyhopping

This is another unique behavior among whales. Spyhopping is when a whale quietly pokes his head just a little out of the water. Then, he slowly turns around, careful not to disturb the water too much. Whale experts believe that whales do this to "spy" on their surroundings (look around without anyone noticing).

Lobtailing

In lobtailing, whales stick their tails out of the water. They swing it around in the air a few times before slapping the surface of the water to create a very loud sound. Why whales do this is still unknown. Some believe that whales do this to warn other whales of danger.

Logging

Logging is when a whale floats motionless just below the surface of the water, like a log. The whale rests while the tail hangs down. While floating motionless, the whale's dorsal fin, parts of the back and of the head can be seen above the water.

Chapter 2 What Are Beluga Whales?

Beluga whales are among the most easily identified kinds of whales. A lot of people often mistake them for their cousins, the dolphins and porpoises.

How does a beluga whale look like?

The adults often have pure white skin. They are small and do not have any dorsal fin (no fin on their backs). The head is broad and round, with a large forehead. They look more like dolphins. Their tails are notched, with flippers that are broad like paddles.

Where does the beluga whale live?

Beluga whales live in colder waters, such as seas and oceans in the arctic and sub-arctic regions. They are a common sight in the waters of Alaska. They are also seen the waters off the coast of Canada, Greenland, Norway and Russia. Because they live in cold parts of the ocean, they have thick blubber layer, as thick as 5 inches. This is to protect their bodies from getting too cold.

What do beluga whales eat?

Beluga whales are among the toothed kind of whales. They eat marine animals that are in season or what is currently abundant in their area. They are called opportunistic feeders, eating whatever is available. They eat salmon, arctic cod, mussels, crabs, octopus, snails, clams, herring, snails, whitefish, rainbow sole, sandworms, char, smelt, tomcod and eulachon.

They look for food on the seabed and in the water column, They usually find food at 1,000 feet deep, but they are also known to dive deeper. They use echolocation, with whistles, chirps and clicks to swim around in search of food or to communicate with other whales.

When do beluga whales reproduce?

They generally swim in groups composed of 2-3 adults to as many as hundreds. Some migrate or travel far while some just swim within a particular area. They can be found very close to the shore or out in the open sea. During the warm summer months, beluga whales swim up into estuaries and rivers to feed and give birth. They mate during the late winter months to early spring. Mother beluga whales give birth after 15 months. Babies swim and feed from their mothers for 2 years.

Baby beluga whales are born with a dark grey color, not like the pure white color of their mothers. As they grow older, their skin color gradually lightens and turns white. When females are 7 years old, their skin color turns into the permanent pure white shade. Males reach their own permanent color when they are 9 years old.

What threatens beluga whales?

Beluga whales are threatened by humans. They are being hunted for food and oil.

Chapter 3 What Are Humpback Whales?

Humpback whales are among the largest kinds of whales. They are baleen whales, meaning they have very fine hair-like structures that serve as filters for food. They are also known for their amazing songs, which are believed to be their way of communicating. They live long lives, usually 45 to 50 years.

What does a humpback whale look like?

The name "humpback" describes the way this whale prepares to dive. It does so by arching its back above the water surface. The humpback whale's head is bulky with a lot of bumps called tubercles. Each bump or tubercle has a bristle. They have 2 blowholes on top of their head.

Their bodies are huge, growing to about 16 meters or 52 feet long. They weigh between 30 to 50 tons. Female humpback whales are a bit larger than males. Their hearts can weigh up to 195 kg or 430 pounds.

Humpbacks come in 4 different skin colors. Some are mottled, some are black, some are white, while some are gray. Their skin often has numerous scars, with patches that are covered with barnacles.

Their tails or flukes have unique white patches. These patches are like fingerprints to them-each humpback's patch is different from the others. The flukes have deep notches and can be as large as 3.7 meters (12 feet) wide. The dorsal fin is small and found near the fluke.

The flippers are huge, which extends to as long as 1/3 of the whale's body. A humpback whale's flippers are the largest among all other kinds of whales. These are white in color, with a mottled appearance. The edges of the flippers are rough. Barnacles may also be found on these flippers.

The throat has14 to 35 grooves that begin from the whale's chin and runs all the way to its navel (bellybutton). These grooves help the whale to expand or open its mouth really wide so it can swallow tons of water. Water that enters the mouth is filtered by the baleen structure, leaving behind tiny sea creatures like plankton for the whale to eat.

What do humpback whales eat?

Humpbacks are seasonal feeders. This means that they eat when their food is abundant. They do not actively hunt. Food for humpbacks includes tiny crustaceans (shelled organisms) like krill, plankton and small fishes like mackerel, sandeel, capelin and herring. Humpbacks can eat an average of 2,000 to 2,500 kg (4,400 to 5,500 pounds) of small fishes, plankton and krill in one feeding season (lasting for 120 days). They feed twice a day during this period.

Humpbacks cooperatively hunt. That means several humpbacks swim together and push their prey towards one area. The concentration of prey makes it easier for the humpbacks to swallow a lot of food in one single gulp. This is called bubble-net type of feeding. Members of the hunting group form a circle as wide as 3.1 to 31 meters (10 to 100 feet) wide and 15 meters (50 feet) deep. This very large area would contain tons of food for these huge whales. Once the prey are herded and concentrated in this area, the humpbacks will blow a bubble wall as they all swim spirally towards the surface. The wall of bubbles traps plankton, small fishes and krill and moves them upwards to the water surface. Once on the surface, the humpbacks start to feed.

There are also about 330 pairs of baleen plates that hang from the whale's jaws. These are dark gray in color, about 0.6 meters (25 inches) long and 34 centimeters (13.5 inches) wide.

What are the activities of humpback whales?

Like most baleen whales, humpbacks usually swim alone. They form temporary groups, usually during feeding season when they perform bubble-net feeding. Only mothers and their babies form strong bonds and swim together for long periods.

Humpbacks are deep divers. They can dive for about 15 to 30 minutes. They can go as deep as 150 to 210 meters (500 to 700 feet).

Breaching is a favorite among humpbacks. They breach high out of the surface of the water and then slap the water as they land back down. Sometimes, humpbacks twirl as they breach. Humpbacks breach for play, to loosen parasites on their skin or communicate.

Spyhopping is also observed among humpbacks. They poke their heads out of the water and look around for about 30 seconds before sinking quietly back into the water.

Lobtailing is also observed in humpback whales. This is more common when the seas are stormy and the waves are rough. Whale experts have yet to find a good explanation why humpbacks do this.

Spouting is likewise observed in humpbacks, which is also common among all other kinds of whales. They breathe through the 2 blowholes on top of their heads. They swim close to the water surface, exposing only these blowholes to the air. They breathe or spout for about 1 to 2 times per minute while they are at rest. After a deep dive, humpbacks spout faster, at 4 to 8 times per minute. When they spout, they blow a double stream of spray straight up into the air, which rises to about 3.1 to 4 meters (10 to 13 feet) high.

These large whales swim at average speeds of 4.8 to 14 kph (3-9 mph). They can also go as fast as 24 to 26.5 kph (15 to 16.5 mph), in bursts, especially when they are in danger. When they feed, they swim much slower, at 1.2 to 3.5 mph.

Do humpbacks sing?

Humpbacks are among the most well known singers. They are the noisiest and the most imaginative. Their songs are very beautiful- long, complex, eerie and varied. These songs contain recognizable grunts, squeaks and other kinds of sounds that flow together in a beautiful song from the deep. Male humpbacks are the only ones that were recorded while singing in warm waters. It is believed that they sing to attract the female humpbacks. When they are in the colder parts of the ocean, male humpbacks can be heard grunting, groaning, scraping and making other rough sounds, very much unlike their melodious songs in the warm seas.

Where do humpbacks live?

Humpbacks are often seen swimming on the surface of the ocean. They live both in the shallow waters bear the coastline and out in the open ocean. They are known to travel long distances, swimming more than 3,100 miles without stopping during their seasonal migration. They travel are 3 to 9 mph or 4.8 to 14 kph. They can swim 1,000 miles in a month.

They travel to the warmer parts of the sea during the mating season and when mother whales are about to give birth. They travel or migrate to the colder waters in order to feed. They usually prefer to swim along shallow waters when they are not migrating. When they are in warm waters, humpbacks do not feed. They rely on their blubber for the energy they need. Baby humpbacks feed on their mother's milk.

There are 3 different groups of humpbacks. One group generally swims in the waters of the North Pacific Ocean. Another group lives in the North Atlantic Ocean. The third group roves the oceans in the Southern Hemisphere.

How do humpbacks reproduce?

Humpback whales breed during the winter months through the early spring, while they are staying near the water surface in the warmer parts of the ocean. Mother whales carry their babies for 11 to 12 months before giving birth. Babies or calves are born near the surface, where the water is warm and shallow. Once born, the calf swims up to the water surface to breathe, within 10 seconds after birth in order to catch its first breath of air. The mother helps her baby to reach t he surface by pushing him gently up using her flippers. Within 30 minutes after he is born, the calf can already swim well. Mother humpbacks generally give birth once every 1 to 3 years.

A humpback calf is born 4.3 meters (14 feet) long. It weighs 2.5 tons. Most humpbacks only give birth to 1 calf at a time.

Although, there have been twins, in about 1% of all humpback births.

Calves swim close to their mothers until they are 1 year old, sometimes longer. They drink their mother's milk and do not feed on sea creatures as the adults do. They can drink as much as 100 pounds of milk every day.

What threatens humpback whales?

There are no natural predators of humpback whales because they are so big. What kill them are humans.

Chapter 4 What Are Blue Whales?

Blue whales are the largest of all whales. They are also the largest animals alive on earth today. They grow to as long as 29 meters or 94 feet, just about the height of a 9-storey building.

What do blue whales look like?

They are so huge and heavy that the weight of their tongue is already as heavy as a full-grown elephant. Their heart weighs as heavy as a car. But despite their massive size, they only eat tiny krill.

What do blue whales eat?

These gigantic creatures eat tiny krill. These are tiny creatures that float around in the oceans and seas. They look like very tiny shrimps. One adult blue whale eats around 3,600 kg of krill each day.

Blue whales catch tiny krill by diving deep into the waters. Blue whales are known to dive as deep as 500 meters in search of food.

They open their mouths very wide to swallow water and then filter it, leaving behind krill and plankton. Each swallow contains around 5,000 kg of seawater. The jaws of the blue whale are lined with a mustache-like fine bristles that filter seawater, as it is forces water out of the mouth. After the water is out of its mouth, the blue whale licks the baleen or bristles to wipe the filtered krill off and swallow it.

Blue whales dive deep to look for food. But they still have to come up to the surface to breathe. They breathe air from a blowhole on top of their heads. When they come up for air, they exhale a cloud of water that rises high up in the air. This cloud of water can shoot out of the blowhole, as high as 9 meters.

Where do blue whales swim?

Blue whales often swim alone. Sometimes they swim in pairs, like a mother blue whale and her baby. They are known to form strong attachments with each other, but never in large permanent groups.

These giant creatures swim gracefully. They can swim to cruising speeds of 8 kph and can go as fast as 30 kph.

Blue whales are among the loudest animals on earth. They talk to each other through moans and groans. Their sounds are so loud that on a good day at sea, they can be heard as far as 1,600 km. Scientists believe that these sounds are for talking to each other as well as to help them find their way in the vast ocean (echolocation).

How do blue whales reproduce?

Mother blue whales give birth to 1 calf every 3 years. They carry their babies for 11 to 12 months before giving birth. Newborn blue whales weigh 2,700 kg and are 8 meters long. Once born, other blue whales help the baby to reach the surface of the water and breathe air. Baby blue whales drink milk from their mothers until they are a year old. They drink as much as 600 liters of milk every day, which help them gain 90 kg every day.

What threatens blue whales?

There aren't many predators or animals that eat blue whales. However, some have been eaten by killer whales and sharks. A lot of these blue whales get injured swimming too close to large ships. They get hit by these passing ships, seriously injuring them. Some even die from these wounds.

Chapter 5 What Are Sperm Whales?

Moby Dick is the most popular sperm whale of all. It is a character in the story written by Charles Dickens- a ferocious beast of the sea hunted by humans. It looked dangerous and fearsome because of its huge head and rows of razor-sharp teeth.

What does a sperm whale look like?

Sperm whales are among the toothed whales. Their skin has a gray color. They have a very large head and their body tapers off towards a much slimmer tail end. Their teeth are sharp and arranged in rows. An adult sperm whale grows up to 67 feet long and weighs almost 56 tons. They have 1 blowhole on top of their head. Their brains are large, weighing about 20 pounds. This is the largest brain in the entire animal kingdom.

Sperm whales are called such because of the oil they produce. This oil is called spermaceti oil. This is produced in the whale's heads.

How do sperm whales behave?

Sperm whales hold the record when it comes to deep diving. It is the deepest diver among all whales. They can easily go as deep as 3,300 feet. Sperm whales form pods and develop very strong bonds with other sperm whales. They are very caring towards their young> they also help their fellow sperm whales who are hurt or sick.

Sperm whales are fond of logging, which make a lot of people think that they are lazy creatures. They are often seen floating motionless right below the water surface. Their tails hang idly down in the water while they float very calmly. They swim at 3 mph but can go at speed bursts of 25 mph when needed.

What do sperm whales eat?

Sperm whales are bottom feeders. They eat food they can find near the ocean floor. Their ability to dive deep helps them find food like eels, fish, octopus and squid. A lot of sperm whales have scars all over their heads. This is believed to be a result of a fight with a squid they are trying to eat. Sperm whales easily eat a ton of food each day.

Often times, the bottom of the ocean is dark. Sperm whales use echolocation to find food, attract prey and to find their way through dark, murky waters.

Where do sperm whales live?

Sperms whales are in most oceans. They swim in both tropical warm waters and in cooler parts of the sea as well.

How do sperm whales reproduce?

Mother sperm whales have babies every 5 years. Their calves drink milk for nearly 2 years. Newborns sperm whale calves are 2 times the length of other newborn whales.

Baby sperm whales already eat squid and other sea creatures while still drinking milk from their mothers. Mother sperm whales help each other in bringing food to their babies because the calves cannot dive deep enough to search for food.

What threatens sperm whales?

People are the biggest threats to sperm whales. They are being hunted for the oil they produce in their heads.

Chapter 6 What Are Right Whales?

Right whales are among the largest kinds of whales. They can be as heavy as 100 tons and grow up to 60 feet long.

What does a right whale look like?

The most unique feature of a right whale is the shape of their blowhole. Other whales have round blowholes on top of their heads. Right whales have V-shaped ones. Their heads also have distinctive calluses. Their bodies are black or dark gray in color. An average right whale weighs 70 tons and is 50 feet long.

Their mouths are very big. On each side of their huge mouth are more than 200 plates, which they use to filter food from the water.

What do right whales eat?

Right whales eat different types of small sea creatures like plankton and krill. They swim slowly with their mouths open, so that water with all the food can enter their mouth. The plates on the sides of their mouth filter the flowing water, trapping food within their structure. They can swim all over the ocean in search for food. They can swim close to the water surface or down at the bottom, wherever they can find food.

How do right whales reproduce?

Male right whales have very large testicles. Scientists believe that the males need to produce large amounts of sperm in order to increase the chances of the female right whales to become pregnant. Female right whales give birth to one calf every 3 to 4 years. They bear their babies for 12 months before giving birth to a bay that's about 20 feet long and weighs almost a ton.

What threatens right whales?

Right whales are among the most hunted kinds of whales. When they die, they float in the water, making it easy for the hunters to gather what they want from the dead bodies. Right whales tend to swim very close to shore, making them very easy targets for hunters. They also swim in places where ships frequently sail. They collide with the ships, suffer serious head injuries, and die. This is why a lot of ships are trying to learn where these whales frequently swim so that they can avoid them.

Right whales can live long lives if they remain protected. They can live between 70 and 100 years old.

Chapter 7 What Are Bowhead Whales?

Bowhead whales are most commonly found in the cold Arctic waters. They are among the most hunted whales over the years. They are among the largest, heaviest whales in the world today, next to blue whales. Bowhead whales are also known as Arctic whale, steeple-top whale, Russian whale Greenland right whale and polar whale.

What does a bowhead whale look like?

The skin of bowhead whales is black, except for a small white patch on the lower front jaw. They grow from 15 to 18 meters long. One bowhead whale grew longer, at 19.8 meters. Full-grown bowhead whales weigh about 75 to 100 tons or about 150, 000 to 200,000 pounds.

One of the most recognizable features of a bowhead whale is the baleen plates they use for filtering water for food. Their skull is large and symmetrical, so large that is about 1/3 of the entire length of their body. They do not have any dorsal fin.

Where do bowhead whales live?

Bowhead whales mostly live in the Arctic region. They swim around the icy waters, along ice-packed areas of the ocean. They also swim to warmer areas in summer, but still within the Arctic region. They would swim in areas where there is no ice when they breed and give birth.

There are 5 known large groups of bowhead whales. Three of them live in the North Atlantic. The other two groups live in the North Pacific region.

How do bowhead whales behave?

Bowheads form small groups, with 2 to 3 other bowhead whales. Most of the time, they prefer to swim alone. During migration, they can form larger groups. Scientists believe that these whales help each other to break through larger chunks of ice in order to reach their destination. Once in areas with fewer or thinner ice, they swim apart and go their own ways.

Like all other whales, bowheads are fond of communicating through songs, groans and squeaks. They can be noisy during migrations, talking to each other.

What do bowhead whales eat?

Bowheads can dive for up to an hour. However, they usually dive in small bursts, each dive lasting for about 15 minutes. They dive to find food, which are tiny sea creatures like krill. They use their baleen for filtering food. They can eat about 100 tons of tiny crustaceans per year. When they feed, they find food in groups, with about 14 other bowheads. They get into a V-formation in search of food.

How do bowhead whales reproduce?

Bowhead whales mate in the late winter season. Females carry their babies for 12 to 14 months before giving birth. Mother bowhead whales give birth to 1 calf every 3 to 4 years. Baby bowhead whales weigh around 2,000 pounds. Calves drink milk and swim with their mothers for 6 to 12 months.

What threatens bowhead whales?

Humans are the main threats to bowhead whales. They have been hunted in the past for their meat and oil. Their blubber and long baleens are also sold.

Conclusion

Thank you again for downloading this book!

I hope you enjoyed reading about my book on whales. These are huge creatures of the earth's waters but are in danger of becoming extinct. Humans are the biggest threats to all kinds of whales. They are being hunted for their blubber or oils and other parts of their bodies. We should all help in creating awareness and in the conservation efforts to save the whales.

Finally, if you enjoyed this book, please take the time to share your thoughts and **post a review on Amazon**. It'd be greatly appreciated!

Thank you!

A Note About The Author

Hathai Ross was born in Thailand and then moved to England in late 2004. She has been writing Books for the past 3 years, mainly on Animals which are her passion.

Feel free to contact Hathai at greenslopesdirect@gmail.com

Check out her Amazon profile Hathai Ross

https://www.amazon.com/-/e/B00JS8EJ52

Next Steps

Please write me an honest review about the book – I truly value your opinion and thoughts and I will incorporate them into my next book, which is already underway.

Check Out My Other Books

Go ahead and check out the other great books I've published!

Snakes: Amazing Facts about Snakes with Pictures for Kids

https://www.amazon.com/Snakes-Amazing-Pictures-Awesome-Creature-ebook/dp/B01MS8VGCH/ref=sr_1_4?s=digital-text&ie=UTF8&qid=1485007306&sr=1-4&keywords=snakes

Dolphins: Amazing Facts about Dolphins with Pictures for Kids

https://www.amazon.com/Dolphins-Amazing-Pictures-Awesome-Creature-ebook/dp/B01M5FFE9G/ref=sr_1_1?s=digital-text&ie=UTF8&qid=1485007555&sr=1-1&keywords=dolphins+hathai

Sharks: Amazing Facts about Sharks with Pictures for Kids:

https://www.amazon.com/Sharks-Amazing-Pictures-Awesome-Creature-ebook/dp/B01MQ48V42/ref=sr_1_8?s=digital-text&ie=UTF8&qid=1485007752&sr=1-8&keywords=hathai+ross

Dinosaurs: Amazing Facts & Pictures for Kids On These Wonderful Creatures

https://www.amazon.com/Dinosaurs-Pictures-Children-Wonderful-Creatures-

ebook/dp/B015AKYH5I/ref=sr_1_1?s=digital-
text&ie=UTF8&qid=1485008081&sr=1-
1&keywords=dinosaurs+for+kids+hathai

Ants: Amazing Facts about Ants with Pictures for Kids

https://www.amazon.com/Ants-Amazing-Pictures-
Awesome-Creature-
ebook/dp/B01M5F041G/ref=sr_1_5?s=digital-
text&ie=UTF8&qid=1485008626&sr=1-
5&keywords=ants+for+kids

Made in the USA
Columbia, SC
19 March 2021